LISTEN

Wisdom from Nature in Poetic Form

Robert James Schout

SCHOUT IT OUT LLC

Listen
Wisdom from Nature in Poetic Form

Publisher
Schout It Out LLC
Wilmington, Delaware

ISBN: 978-1-959168-16-4

Library of Congress Control Number: 2024917634

First Edition

For more information about the author and other books and products by Robert James Schout and Schout It Out LLC, visit: www.schoutitout.com

To order copies of this book in digital, hardcopy, or audio formats, visit: www.schoutitout.com

ACKNOWLEDGMENTS

To the writers and poets who came before me. Thank you for inspiring all of us to see Nature in all her glory. To scientists of nature. Thank you for insights into our destructive nature and healing possibilities. To environmental activists and preservationists. Thank you for stirring the heads, hearts, and hands of millions into action in countless ways.

To my Leandro.
Each time we step outside, take a drive, or explore this incredible planet, while spreading your arms in a grand expanse, you say, "My Love, I give this to you." You remind me of the incredible beauty that always surrounds me. You invite me to stop dwelling upon busy thoughts and turn my attention and gratitude to nature's gifts, from the importance of a bee or butterfly to the majesty of a mountain, sea, or tree. Thank you, my love, for being nature's gift to me.

To Nature, herself.
We are one in being with everything. In your constancy, you speak to us in every form. Every sentient being shares lessons with us. You whisper to us, scream at us, show us everything there is to know about life and living itself: beauty, fragility, strength, inevitable cycles, prosperity, and limitations to be accepted. Our role is to witness, honor, steward, learn, preserve, and protect. Thank you for this oneness of being.

INTRODUCTION

The year was 1978. I walked into a classroom for what I hoped would be a "blow-off" optional English class. I registered for the class to receive extra course credit on my high school transcript. The class was Western European and Early American Poetry. I thought, "I'll read some boring verse that I probably won't understand. Kiss up to the teacher. Engage in my best acting expressions and get an 'A' in the class." The text was *The Norton Anthology of Poetry*—more than 500 pages of poetry and poetic prose. It became one of the most pivotal courses that I took in high school. The text, the teacher, the verses made me fall in love with poetry, with song, with the nature of things, and with love itself. It helped open my eyes and mind to multiple perspectives on love, life, inner and outer turmoil, nature, all forms of beauty, and more.

It would be many decades before I put pen to paper and began scribbling basic verse outside of a classroom; sometimes simple rhymes, poetic prose, other forms of free verse – even a sonnet and haiku would be scribbled on Post-it notes and filed in a box. All poems were secrets, shared as whispers between me and Nature herself.

Nature would be my first muse. She would whisper to me on wisps and gusts of wind. She would drip philosophical truths into my mind with each raindrop. She would invite me to lay upon her soft breast covered by green grass, moist moss, or dry dirt. She would allow me to hear her heartbeat from deep within her earthen body and ask me to write about time passing. She would listen as I walked along isolated paths, speaking to her of loneliness, desperate dreams, lost and confused feelings, hope, and love. She would compassionately, silently listen as I screamed at her and out to her from mountain peaks. She would listen as I would pose hundreds of questions to her about life's assurance, promises, wonders, and fears. Along what seems now like a million miles of walks, my mind and tongue would still themselves. Talking would cease. Upon pebbled paths, within forested glen, and on icy peaks, she invited me into her silence. She would speak to me, and I would listen.

This is why I go, still, to the wilderness of a city, suburb, desert, or mountain path so often. In parks, along sidewalks, leaning against a tree, tilling the soil in a garden, witnessing life pushing itself through a crack in some concrete, sitting by the seaside, or meandering along a mountain trail. Everywhere she is present, and her voice can be heard if we just stop, look, and listen. I'm a tree-hugger because trees speak. I stop to touch, smell, and gaze upon flowers for hours because every flower is the essence of her, reaching out to entreat, mesmerize, and beckon each of us to stop and set our mind upon the beauty in our midst. Her beauty is not to be plucked, stolen from her grasp, but to be tenderly touched, nurtured, or simply noticed. I'm a person who walks down unmarked paths because they carry a person for mere meters or miles into her wonderland, and I trust her to keep me safe and lead me home.

We are all in a state of inter-being: one in being with everything, everywhere, all the time. This includes all of Nature. She whispers and, sometimes, screams for our attention as a giver and sustainer of life and a co-being of life itself. Found within this collection, in simple or dramatic verse, free-form or structured sonnet, haiku, or rhyming couplet, Nature shares her wisdom. She implores and entreats us to slow down and live life, to consider things of real importance. She invites us to notice cycles of life and to learn from that which grows around us and sustains every breath we take. All things in nature offer lessons in fact or metaphoric form.

Regardless of the form, natural messenger, or note, she is constantly saying, "Listen."

So, my friends, I invite you to read even the simplest of verses. Reflect on what She conveys. Through the verses offered within this book, listen to Her.

- Robert J. Schout

Contents

PART I

LISTEN TO THE SUN

The Breath of Dawn

Awaken to dawn.

Her breath warm, piercing the darkness,

coaxing its blanket of shadow to retreat and release its grip,

cold and foreboding to some, comforting to others,

as they unwrap themselves from their isolated slumber.

Her breath warm and gentle,

caressing the sprigs of body hair protruding from soft,

well-worn skin,

textured by decades of days,

tingling, mingling, dancing on a dermis born to live,

inviting it to awaken, rise with excitement,

sun-drenched by a new day.

Her breath warm and light, kissing cheeks,

retracing the memories of laugh lines of days gone by,

exploring the emerging relentless crevices that prove a life lived,

with new days yet to dawn.

In stillness, she breathes her warm breath,

as the world awakens and considers new paths and possibilities,

opportunities for peace that stream into consciousness,

attached ever so lightly to each ray

on the horizon of this new day.

Thoughts flitter and float.

Flights of fancy dissolve like mist in the mind

as dawn's breath, gentle, warm, peaceful, and light,

gives way to tentative, worrisome gasps, in fear of life, for air.

The day has begun.

Oh, how I yearn for the next breath of dawn.

IN THE SHADOWS OF THE MORN

In the shadows of the morn

a trail reaches out and pulls at my pantleg.

Though the world's eyelids open,

unable to slumber while luminescence expands,

secret ponds spring from unseen submerged fountainheads

on a still darkened path.

Arbors harbor hidden views of life's plenitude

encountered only as the sounds of twigs and grounded leaves

that crackle in the underbrush,

moved by creatures not yet visible to naked eyes.

Passages through thickets where most fear to tread,

afraid of the slightest barb that might pierce

the fragile hopes and transient dreams held tightly to their breasts, reveal the strength of nature's will within us,

offering transcendent, universal truths,

from a billion of our brethren's souls in miniature form

buzzing, crawling, slithering, and scampering

through the woodlands, fluttering on a breeze,

holding nature's irrevocable wisdom just off the pedestrian path:

"Be what you were created to be.

Persistently move, adapt, change, grow,

and slow, when necessary,

surrendering to forces you can't control.

You're alive, so fully live."

All lessons can be learned along this path

in the shadows of the morn.

*2017 Winner of Ross Andrews Nature Poem Contest.

WHY DOES THE SUN RISE?

Why does the sun rise?

> To make sweet love. To awaken a body ever so slowly with each warm breath. Inhaling and exhaling as it travels the length of mountained spines and across fruited plain. Coming close. Opening its radiant arms. Breathing its warm moist breath. Extending its ecstatic kiss into dew as it trails its tongue of light across the dermis of savannahed plains.

Why does the sun rise?

> To brush twined vines dense in forested dew with moist sundrenched breath. Heating them until vapors rise to rain the sweat that will cool the body above and below. Forcing the midnight frost to scurry and retreat in grace and in fear of evisceration, as forests cheer their knight's arrival, freeing them from cocooned isolation.

Why does the sun rise?

To silently, ravenously mingle with waters, matching each rhythm and flow, penetrating the depths of rivers and streams, oceans, and seas, warming them, making water rise. Reminding water that it too is of the sky, destined to dissolve and evaporate into new life of clouds and rain. As it is called home; it, too, remembers that it is one with the sun.

Why does the sun rise?

To receive the gratitude of reflected praise as a firmament of stars, reflections of itself, twinkle upon the waves, and in steady streams from springs as the sun bids farewell 'til morrow.

LOVE LIKE THE SUN

Love – like the rising of the sun.

Allow it to burst forth in your heart and blaze in your mind,

> Shining through your eyes
>
> Settling upon your tongue
>
> Radiating from your touch

Streaming outward

> Warming a heart
>
> Helping a friend
>
> Healing a soul.

KISSED BY SUNLIGHT

To strangers this talk may seem trite,

luminescent yet transparent insight.

At my side day and night,

as I walk, I am kissed by sunlight.

Strolling along silent paths and singing trees,

peace unfolds as a mind's eye sees,

nymphs and fairies dancing on a breeze,

elves and centaurs frolicking amongst the leaves.

There, my spirit resides.

There, where freedom be and no fear hides.

Come and linger at my side,

and with wild abandon we'll abide.

In Autumn

There are a few days

when you can capture rays

of sunlight in your veins,

but you must release the reins

that hold you to seasons

for selfish reasons,

to become one

with the sun.

SUNSET

Watching, softly in sweet repose,

heart awakening as the sunset rose.

Mesmerized by strokes of artistic design,

brushed with the hand of the Divine.

Eyes transfixed, heart afire,

oneness of Being, its grandeur inspires.

Consumed by wonder of eternity,

a mind outstretched to infinity.

PART II

LISTEN TO THE WATERS

DROPLETS OF WATER

A droplet of water does not pine to be an ocean,

nor does it seek to become a lake.

It does not work to form itself into a sculpture of artistic ice,

to dazzle onlookers with its beauty.

It does not try to quench the thirst of people

nor nurture a plant's life.

It does not yearn to traverse canyons, arroyos, or riverbeds,

seeking to explore distant lands above and below,

nor to test itself upon the rocks and falls

that it encounters along its way.

It does not strive for ego's sake to dazzle you

by dancing on a flower's edge,

nor feel an ounce of timidity

as it shelters silently in secret cenotes.

This droplet of water that I see, simply flows and forms,

saying *yes* to the requests made of it,

by earth, wind, sky, and unseen forces

made by and unknown to man,

allowing itself to be molded and transfigured by trail and time,

into rain and rivers,

oceans and storms,

ice and snow,

springs and mist,

clouds and fog.

It bows to elemental forces,

allowing itself to be used, consumed,

formed, and transformed,

to sustain that which is,

and bring forth that which can be.

These droplets of water, so plentiful and pristine,

beckon me to bend and bow to forces unseen,

inviting me to wonder,

"What is it that I can be?"

Rain

Look,   see the ashened face of your mother.

Her light present,   behind.

For today, see she cries;

tears of hope pour, raining down.

Each droplet shed to wash away the dirt and grime

of sadness, desperation, and grief

that lay upon the faces

and muddy the hearts of her children.

Let her tears of love wash away the sins of yesterday,

cleansing the slate of today.

Her torrent of tears merely meant to refill wells that have run dry,

emptied of hope, courage, and joy.

Go!

Stand in her mist, let it refresh and fill you.

See,   her tears collect in pools upon humanity's body,

seeping into its soul,

lingering in puddles to be lapped up by those

who fail to catch her tears upon their tongues.

Come!   Wade into her river of life,

let her life stream trickle into your mind and quench your thirst.

Come!   Taste her water, bathe in her love.

And when there seems to be none left,   stand in her stillness,

extending your roots down, deep into her body

where life flows in hidden streams just beneath the surface,

nurturing the roots of humanity's love so that life can spring eternal.

Mother,   rain down your tears,

as we open our mouths and our minds,

pressing our lips to the sky,

to catch every last drop of your wisdom and love,

so that we may live   again.

CASCADAS

Centuries pass.

Civilizations and cultures,

like granite walls neatly laid, rise and fall.

Figures who twisted and turned a lifetime upside down, die.

And the water continues to cascade over the falls,

oblivious to it all.

Tyrants rise and fall.

Wars, waged for egoic reasons, rage.

Millions senselessly suffer.

And the water continues to cascade over the falls,

oblivious to it all.

Our love blossomed and grew.

Ravaged by emotional winds,

pulled apart and back together year after year.

Each eternally mattered to the other

in every moment of this lifetime.

But the waters continue to cascade over the falls,

oblivious to us all.

Aqua Therapy

Is water aggressive or assertive?

Is it bound to change its emotional rhythmic pace and tone

at the whim of the forms and forces that shape or channel it?

Is its temperament based on the channels

through which it must flow?

Is the molecular nature of water, in solemn form,

or multiplied in multitudes,

the dynamic essence of emotion itself?

Is it capable of softness?

Moist as a kiss of morning dew?

Aggressing when it is upheaved?

Strengthened when stressed and pushed through narrows?

Deadened when confined and darkened?

Assertive when torrents of need or deluges of dreams flow?

Gentle when sprung from a single source that meanders through

terrain seemingly carved uniquely for a single conscious stream?

Or still and settled when the surrounds have cared for themselves

and the water itself has found peace upon a bed beneath?

Let no one shame a water's force or form if they have not flowed

through the same terrain. Remember that it is adapting to the

elements around and within. Accept it without bias.

Simply help it settle or flow as it was meant to be.

THE SEA

Waves crash upon my heart's shore,

making violent love to me.

Washing me, scraping, and scouring

the jagged emotional stones that have protected

and fortified me from slipping and dissolving

into an ocean of bliss.

I surrender to the tidal forces of burgeoning passion

within my heart, mind, soul, and loins,

allowing the waves of your hands, lips, and love

to erode the man-made shoreline

that has provided a false protection for my feelings.

I look out, past my shore, to the horizon near,

and yearn to be one, once more, with the sea.

PART III

LISTEN TO THE TREES

WE THE TREE

I am you in kind.

You see me differently.

Yet Aspen roots are one.

AMONGST THE JUNIPERS AND PINES

Amongst the junipers and pines,

on a dusty red rock gardened slope,

where the billions of nature's creatures and I sit,

there, in the pristine silence, I hear all.

I see the bustle of a universe and its creatures,

hitherto fore unnoticed by human eye,

scampering about in a world of their own,

graciously oblivious to all but the timbers and the slope.

I hear the breath of nature,

Mother Earth inhaling and exhaling

her love for all life,

her winded voice whispering in my ear.

Attuned to the echo of the Universe,

Its rhythmic hum pulsating through my being,

I too become one with its vibration,

I am still.

I feel the peace of heaven on this earth.

I see that we are all one,

all intertwined in the fabric of life.

On this slope, amongst the junipers and pines,

I know God.

*First published in *Sacred Journeys*, 2007

ASPENS AT THE EDGE OF WINTER

standing in the cemetery on the hill

among the hundreds of markers unknown

that rise like spires to the sky.

some scribbled with fragments from children's minds

who, in blissful ignorance, deface the afterlife.

some with the initials of lovers grasping at eternal remembrance.

some bearing witness by their weathered, worn, textured skin:

the sights and seasons and ages of sun.

each marker, a reminder of life lived.

oh, how we gloried in your birth as if it heralded our own,

giving us permission to live,

reminding us of our strength to emerge from cocoons

cloaked in darkness,

like seeds covered by cold and snow,

belying the life that is waiting within.

how we casually took for granted your

canopy of comfort,

the strength of your arms

and the gentleness of your breath

as it cooled us during our seasons in the sun.

how we were awed and mesmerized

by the cathedrals of color

that you created in the twilight of seasons past

relishing every moment in your midst,

hoping that you would hold on just a bit longer

so that we could rest in your wisdom and bask in your beauty.

now, all we can see are nameless,

faceless markers on hillsides

barely noticed by passersby, who,

caught up in their own weary worlds,

fail to honor your presence or stop long enough

to hear your still, soft voices whispering in the breeze

calling out for us to remember.

TREE HOUSE

Each leaf tossed and twisted by cyclones

invisible to the naked eye,

in minute proportions.

Created by a wind whipped miles away.

Working with the Earth and sky in a partnership eons old.

Each flick and flutter unleashes power

of hurricane proportion in microscopic form,

cleansing the cluttered space of this tree house.

CUPBOARDS

A chill still drapes the air.

Winter's blanket slowly receding.

Folded and tucked away for another day, seasons from now.

Replaced by the fresh linen of Spring,

Taken out of the cupboards.

Unfolded, shaken in the breeze, and laid out,

As buds in the trees.

A MOST PERFECT PLACE

It is a most perfect place,

to fully face,

all that is held inside this space.

With trembling hands,

my heart precipitously expands,

to relinquish my façade's egoic demands.

Mother merely waves her arms to capture my gaze,

begging me to step through mind-numbing haze,

to witness possibilities, a range that limitless lays.

Leaves call out as we play in the sun.

The time for work and thought is done.

A world awaits, a dream is spun.

Here, now, do I aspire,

and set my soul afire,

to inhale and live with fervent desire,

to continuously be,

surrounded by thee,

together as one, for eternity.

MARKERS OF LIFE

Standing patiently

marking a mountain of life

bearing scars and wounds that stretch over time.

Easily weathering cold and storms

with veins cut and carved occasionally

by the knives of self-centered youth

hoping that they will be remembered by all.

You bear their mark,

their hope, their stain of conceit

long after they return to the earth,

until their grandchildren come along.

You endure admiration, awed inspiration

and ignorance, proudly, patiently

standing, simply knowing that life

is meant to live, sharing messages

only you can give.

THE TREES KNOW

They have learned to rest, to stop, to allow their roots to stand firm in their Mother's strength. They have learned to suckle on the tits and drink of the milk of their Mother, absorbing, sharing, and returning life.

They have learned that doing takes a back seat to Being. That to bend too far is to break. So, break gently with the world. Simply, uniquely, be. That is enough to merit existence and happiness.

They've learned that nothing lasts forever, except time itself. That the sun and stars will traverse the skies, and that creation will continue long after they have gone. That the tides will ebb and flow, seeming to infinity, a dream we hold, to contrast with our temporal presence.

They've learned that time will come and take them away. They have learned that living and dying are one and the same. Everything exists in an eternal cycle. That all things pass only to be reborn. If one waits long enough, they will surely witness life in unending regenerative form, inspiring hope and releasing fear in all.

They have learned that giving is receiving, and will happen regardless of request, offer, or demand. Because of inter-being, all is dependent on everything. Each will strive for what it needs and offer what it can.

They have learned to be life itself. To be green, to be seen, and to sigh with sadness as we speed on by. Most of all, they have learned to worry-not and want-not. They have learned to simply be grateful, graceful, and life-giving.

They beg me to sit and wonder, *What else can I learn from trees?*

HERE I STAND

All manner of storms have I weathered.

All seasons have I sojourned and still I stand.

The parched earth cradles my roots,

squeezing every last drop of its life into me,

hoping that I will be the one to remain strong in its strength

on these rocky slopes awash with dusted winds and rain.

There are others, scattered here and there,

clinging to dear life, by the thread of steadfast faith,

rising from countless deaths that have come before.

Daring the world to challenge their will,

persistence, and fortitude.

Thunder on the mountain in the distance

reminds all of impending storms and seasonal shifts

that will always come.

All manner of beasts intuit their vulnerability.

They scurry for shelter, fearing the feeling of a world

in temporary disarray and chaos.

Yet I remain, waiting, yearning for these winds of change

and the reign of good fortune to come and shower me,

with its substance and streams that will ensure endurance and life.

I fear not the winds and rain,

nor the rocky slopes,

for my roots are embedded deep within the earth

as I stretch with open arms toward the sky.

See me, for here I stand.

SKIN FLAKES

Your parched sunbaked skin

peels back with each breeze,

revealing a fresh, well-worn epidermis of life;

protecting, hydrating, caring, and baring your smooth, hard underbelly,

Even in the blistering heat, you offer sweetness

Fruit from blushed berries dangle before eyes,

Drop into my hand and stain the underside of my feet

as they stand beneath your shade.

A piece of you peels off in the breeze, reaching out,

floating to me, settling upon my chest.

You, a part of me, mingle for a few moments in intimacy, both

realizing the value and brevity of life as a wind takes you away.

PART IV

LISTEN TO THE MOUNTAINS

Ocean Summit

If you climb high enough,

you can hear waves of sky crash and crest upon peaks.

The currents crash against granite embankments,

lap the tree line, erode the muscle, Earth has raised,

exposing her tender roots and tundra'd stories hidden for eons.

The waves sweep you and steep you simultaneously

in insignificance and wonder.

Minute by minute, for eternity, the waves crash and winds whip

the rock-walled faces. Sand blasts new skin along this terrain.

Currents continue on high. The ocean's sound deafening at 12,000 feet.

I once held a shell to my ear.

I could hear the ocean within a meadow.

Now, I tell you, if you climb high enough,

the sound of waves are carried upon the wind

and the sea can be heard in thee.

ROCKS AND STONES

The path is strewn with stones, crushed and well worn.

An offering from Mother Earth to come, step further.

Trust more. Discover.

Steady, stable, and firm under foot.

It is a promise of the solidity of substance of Her, in you.

An invitation to walk on.

Rocks, jagged stones on all sides, unearthed,

cast down from on high and upheaved from below.

A garden of edges pave a path with beauty, doubt, and intrigue,

beckoning all who dare, to brave the wilderness about and within.

Come. Wander from walkways manicured and pristine,

populated by well-coiffed, perfectly positioned paved stones,

offering the illusion of control and assurance.

Climb higher, off the trail, into the unknown,

where the Earth makes its own way.

This earth, in and around you,

littered with rocks and stones,

carvings of continuous evolution,

the debris of remembrance of what was

once hidden underground.

Though not visible to the rushed eye or wandering mind,

the beauty of this sacred landscape,

around and within,

is apparent to those who stop, step off the path,

and fear not an occasional stumble or stubbed toe.

Tiers of eons past are etched in stone, reminding us that we, too,

will be remembered by her.

Amongst the rocks, new life emerges from fallen timbers.

Saplings use strength to push through the rough and ragged soil.

This hardened, well-worn surface belies the depth of being.

These rocks and stones hint of the reality of being:

the solidity, determination, and unstoppable nature of life.

.

MOUNTAIN MOTHER

Sitting next to an open vein,

a breath away from the slow, steady flow

of her clean, clear, transluscent blood,

watching as it courses from her body,

upon which I am cradled,

I become one with her.

Her sparkling, effervescent life streams forth before my eyes,

moistening her dark skin, soft to the touch, my fingers dance in the dirt,

smiling as she covers my skin, seeping under my nails.

I brush the lush trestles of her emerald hair,

cascading and flowing gently down her sloped wooded brow,

where eyes see all.

She invites me to lay upon her bosom,

and across her belly

strength and softness surround and enfold me.

her wooded arms reach out above inviting the sun and sky

to bathe me as she caresses me with bird song and butterflies

wisped on a gentle breeze in her trees.

I hear her heartbeat.

Her cool, clear blood springs crystalline

from deep within her moss-covered sheath.

Singing a sweet melody as it trickles and ripples

down the ridges of her mountainous breasts,

following lifelines from long ago,

to carry life, across her well-worn skin

in between the crevices of her rocky fingers.

I reach out and taste and am revived by her.

My eyes trace her body in universal dimension.

I see beyond the horizon of human mind.

Her canyons are rich in natural splendor.

The bush and barrow of her thighs for a dozen miles

cradle new life, giving safe refuge to all that learn

to wrap itself in her living womb.

FROM THEIR OLYMPIC PERCH

From their Olympic perch

do the gods of man still rend their whims upon the Earth?

Do they give casual thought to the

turbulent activity of unconscious sentient societies?

Do they even notice us?

Or do they say, "Let us just stay,

quiet, humble, and strong.

They will be gone before long."

Do they sit stoically knowing that

the joys of life are whittled away

by ages of rain, wind, and change?

Knowing that nothing is lost, merely transformed?

Do they notice the little ones scurrying about,

in their mundane matters of myopic life?

The gods, if they still be, smile silently, reflecting on eternity,

knowing that only moments matter and then they don't.

These gods of Earth, in mankind's mind,

guardians of the ages, overseers of time and change,

wise in their steadfast stillness, moved only minutely by eons,

notice only how long eternity lasts, and its meaning.

PART V

LISTEN TO THE EARTH

REST AWHILE

Slow down dear one, and rest a while

at my side.

In the midst of your frantic, frenetic pace,

life passes you by

and will end,

all too soon.

So, stop, dear one, and rest awhile.

Sit a moment by my side,

and notice with me,

the bliss of simply being,

The colors of the sky.

The early morning dew.

The sounds of life

surrounding you.

The silence of the trees.

The turning of the tide,

The freshness of a breeze

at my side.

All is missed,

as you speed on by.

So, sit, dear one and

rest, awhile.

ONE STEP AT A TIME

The mind, like the Earth, is made for traversing.

No land, sea, space, or sound is out of bounds.

No points, nor places, were created for us, not to go.

We were made to explore inner and outer worlds,

discovering and uncovering our heavens on Earth.

There are no mountains above or below uninvited to ascend.

No gullies nor canyons that we cannot cross.

No forests primeval too dark to discover.

No rivers we cannot wade through.

Nor oceans we cannot sail.

No valleys too deep, nor cliffs too steep.

No meadows hidden with peace behind,

that we are not meant see and find.

No hills too high, nor rocks too jagged,

that will not offer themselves as hand holds, foot holds,

ladders along the pathways of life

steadying our step and giving us rise.

No roads too long, paths too worn,

weather to storm, ice too cold,

seas too deep, deserts too barren,

that we will not find refuge from and within.

The very Earth and all of its inhabitants,

small and large, animate, and inanimate,

breathe reassurance, created as companions,

clear our paths, show us the way,

support us, mingle among us, joining us

on wing and foot along the way,

for a while or a day,

reminding us that we are never alone.

We traverse the Earth as we do life,

one step,

one question,

one answer,

one yes,

one willingness to push on and forge ahead,

with thoughts of *I Can, Why Not*, and *Let Go.*

One step at a time it happens,

this ascension, this discovery.

And so, another step it is that I shall take.

Natural Observations

Mingle, frolic, float, and fly,

on the wings of a bird or gentle butterfly.

Chancing life's possibilities,

as you dance, and sing, taunt, and tease.

Sharing space with ants and bees

barely noticed from the trees.

All, together, in one place,

some to rest, some to chase.

A family of life, one with all

in winter, spring, summer, fall.

Loving all as sisters and brothers,

seeing and honoring the lives of others.

Now is the chance for all mankind,

to lift the veil of ignorance, blind

and seize the day, abandoned and free,

expressing each personal liberty.

Woven together in a tapestry,

bound together in destiny.

Each with an inalienable spiritual right.

Each important to life for light.

SPRING FORTH IN WINTER

a bud pushes forth in the midst of winter

a sign of strength and determination

rising through the darkness

life's sight transfixed on but one end, embracement of light

inside volcanic energy swirls

felt by one in motion

commanding it in silence to rise and stretch

to show itself and stretch to the sun

its birth shrouded in wonder, joy, and worry

will the winter give way so that this bud can be cradled

will its fragility and strength allowed to exist

rush my darling, open, unfurl your petals and leaves

catch the sun and wind quickly before you are noticed by the fowl

before the frost returns from its slumber

rise, open, swallow rivers and waterfalls of sacred life

digest it, let it fill you with life-giving force

for winter may return soon in temporary surprise

shocking your system, blunting your hopes of pleasant days

no harm is meant by these knives of nature

but cuts may ensue, and you may be scarred

remember to always return to the light

look up and out from within

bud and blossom, push and provoke excited

tease and taunt the world with all that can be

even in the midst of winter, rise, and I will notice you.

WINTER'S MAIDEN

Oh, beautiful Lady.
See her as she enters
the horizoned ballroom
in her gown of white.
Crystalline sequins illuminate,
calling attention to her presence,
glistening in the light,
flying through the air
as she dances on the wind.
Sequins fly high and far.
We run to catch them
with outstretched tongues
and for a moment
we become her consort.
Kissing her,
drawn to her,
opening our arms,
we enter the dance.

Fly Like a Butterfly

Do you know where you're going?

Do you know where you've been,

my little floating friend?

What is it you seek?

What will you find,

as you leave your cocoon of darkness behind?

Searching, seeking something new,

something inside,

calling you.

Beckoning you to,

leading you fro.

not knowing which way to go.

Stay true to yourself.

Continue your quest.

The time is not for you to rest.

Listen carefully, and be so true,

to the soft, quiet voice

inside of you.

Continue to look,

for you will find,

life's treasures so sweet and sublime.

APPRECIATE

Why tolerate what we should appreciate?

Do not bridle one's heart, instead unbind one's mind.

The black orchid is not to be picked,

but to entrance and inspire awe.

Stamens are pollinated

by innocuous sexes in order to breed new life.

Young saplings silently linger

among ancient elders in the forest.

A tattered and torn pedal after a storm

does not scream to be plucked but its strength to be admired.

The butterfly migrates across southern miles

to be welcomed not bounded by man-made borders.

Our earthen-mother and spirited sky have no dogma or doctrine

but love, care, and oneness of all.

Each is called to appreciate nature within and around, above and below,

and the temporal tides that wash away the self.

THE DEATH OF BEAUTY

Are we biased against beauty,

merely tolerating autumn hues

in the firmament of endless sky?

Should bigotry extend to blades of grass,

so that roots of blue become

viciously barred from refuge

amongst verdant green glades?

Shall we scapegoat the spirals or petals of a sunflower,

brushing away bees,

forbidding the nectar-tasting of these

colored ones?

Might we allow floralism and faunism to rage

in increasingly concretized landscapes,

until a rarified sight of a raccoon in a shadowed park

causes us to dart away?

See how our stereotypes extend even to winged doves:

the symbol of which now stirs fear

in boundaried and bordered antiquated minds.

One leads to the other, reinforcing another.

Tolerance of bias allows for bigotry,

Bigotry for scapegoats

Scapegoats for stereotypes

Stereotypes for isms

Isms for outright fears

Fears for boundaries

Boundaries for perpetual borders

The death of beauty may stem from a strain of tolerance.

SIRENS

Who are these sirens whose song is heard in forested glen,

offering wisdom and dreams rustled amongst leaves?

Mother Earth in a myriad of forms.

Each diminutively stands before bodies,

breaking, bleeding, shivering, crumbling at their core.

Strong in essence and form.

The sunlight of assurance set on high beams,

streams from her eyes, her silent song, carried on a breeze, disappearing

amongst the trees.

Laced with ancient wisdom,

drawing us near to her heart.

Deeper into the woods, I follow the sirens' song.

REMEMBER ME

Lying upon her trestles, green, coarse,

dry from too much sun,

sinking into the blackened soil of her skin,

parched to the touch,

reddened by perspired rock

awash from her mountain breasts,

mingling with remnants of life before mine,

whose death has offered new life,

I offer my essence to give her hope,

willing to dissolve into nothingness over time,

forgotten by all mankind.

I wonder,

will she remember me once she consumes me?

Eternal Connection

Like a wave unto the ocean, and a raindrop in a storm,

Like a grain of sand upon a beach, I am simply a matter of form.

Like a ray of light at sunrise, and mist in a cloud,

Like a smile on a face, or a voice in a crowd.

Like fawns in a forest, and birds in the trees,

Like fish in the waters, I am each of these.

Like blood unto the body, like thoughts born of mind,

Like feelings of the heart, I am each and every kind.

You are to me, a part of the great expanse,

a part of a greater love, a part of a greater dance.

You are the echo in the wind, the spring about to start,

The ground beneath your feet, of this you are a part.

We inter-are as one. We cannot come apart.

Forever we are one, in body, mind, and heart.

EPILOGUE

All life is one. We inter-are with everything, everywhere, at all times. Intersectionality of issues and challenges, interconnections between people and cultures, interrelationships between happenings around the world and in history are causal. None are coincidental. All of these things are manifestations of a deeper, universal truth. The truth of interbeing.

I and the trees and streams are one. You and the mountains and oceans are one in being. We and the animals, insects, and plants of all kinds, everywhere, are all one in being. It matters not whether I am a mountain or meadow, deer or fawn, some type of flora or fauna, woman, man, any gender, or other beautiful creation on this planet. All life is inseparable, intertwined at all times, in destiny.

Because of this truth, all life, all things can teach us, comfort us, support us, speak to us: in metaphor and analogy, in energy and sustenance, in language and intuitive exchange, in infinite ways. Each form possesses a function. All interlocked in destiny with all other forms. Part of one body, one future, one life.

Carefully consider choices and actions. To maliciously harm even the smallest sprig of grass for egoic gain or selfishly steal away and unnaturally alter terrain for self-centered reasons is to destroy a piece of yourself, a piece of our collective being. The world is designed to nurture and support all life. Every insect, breath, droplet has a reason and purpose. No single form or manifestation is more important than another, no matter what our minds, tribalistic cultures, or dogmatic texts may say.

How should beings survive and thrive without water or breathe without trees…billions of them? Every plant has a purpose. Should the fish of the oceans and streams or birds of the skies be hunted for sport – death reaped upon species in a chain of life for the ego, fun, and pastime dalliance of a few humans?

As interbeings, the clarion call of our age is to actively be with, not just in, the world in which we co-exist. As interbeings, we have the hands and resources to repopulate forests in our neighborhoods, yards, towns, and cities. We have the knowledge, seeds, spaces, and power on community councils to replace decorative gardens that cannot harbor life with natural gardens, flowers, and plants that beckon life to return.

Nature is whispering to each of us at all times. Sometimes, she screams. Listen to her. She will comfort, educate, guide, nourish, and provide. Remember, we are one – interbeing with her – listen to her, then heed her words.

ABOUT THE AUTHOR

Robert Schout – poet, author, column contributor to newspapers and journals, business consultant, personal/professional life coach, leadership and management skills expert, and organization effectiveness specialist – believer in dreams. Robert Schout has dedicated his life to service, first as a social worker, then visiting professor, spiritual teacher, organization consultant and executive coach, and now as an author and poet. He has heard the voice and words streaming into consciousness of dozens of books and hundreds of poems over the years, always taking notes, scribbling words and phrases to remember, on thousands of pieces of paper. Finally completing collections of nature poems, spirit-inspired poetry, and LGBTQ poetry, and offering them, as he has his service, to the world.

Explore other books and inspirational products by Robert Schout
by visiting www.schoutitout.com

Schout It Out LLC Publications and Products

Published poems by Robert James Schout

Timeless Voices, 2005
- "Let Me Hide"

Sacred Journeys, 2007
- "Amongst the Junipers and Pines"

Scenes from the Live Poet's Society, 20th Anniversary, Vol. IV, 2011
- "The Breath of Dawn"
- "Restless Gaze"
- "Rain"
- "God's Answer"
- "Droplets of Water"

2017 Winner: Ross Andrews Nature Poem Contest – "In the Shadows of a Morn"

Schout It Out LLC Publications and Products

I Can Illustrated Children's Books

- *What Can I See Today*
- *What Can I Do Today*
- *What Can I Say Today*
- *What Can I Give Today*

Light Stream: Spirit-Inspired Poetry and Poetic Prose

Turning and Returning: Guided Meditations for Gaining Insight. (Audio Book)

Schout It Out Greeting Card Collections
- Winter Scenes Collection
- Piece of Heaven Collection
- Street Art Collection
- Sea Life Collection
- Coloring Card Collection for Kids

Visit *Schout It Out LLC* for more information
www.schoutitout.com
schoutitout@gmail.com

PowerSkills Training & Development Inc Seminars and Services

Rob Schout is President of PowerSkills Training & Development, Inc.

PowerSkills Everywhere Seminars

PowerSkills offers more than 50 online and onsite courses and seminars focused on a wide range of professional, organization, and management development skills.

PowerSkills Micro-Training Classes

PowerSkills offers micro-training classes on a variety of professional development, leadership development, life skills, and life-enrichment lessons and strategies.

PowerSkills Coaching and Advising

PowerSkills offers personal growth, professional goal achievement, management insight-orientation, and executive advisory coaching services by its team of certified coaching professionals.

Visit *PowerSkills Inc.* to request copies of catalogs
www.powerskillsinternational.com
info@powerskillsinternational.com